STUNT DRIVING

RACE CAR LEGENDS
COLLECTOR'S EDITION

A.J. Foyt

The Allisons

Dale Earnhardt Jr.

Danica Patrick

Famous Finishes

Famous Tracks

The Jarretts

Jeff Burton

Jeff Gordon

Jimmie Johnson

Kenny Irwin Jr.

The Labonte Brothers

Lowriders

Mario Andretti

Mark Martin

Monster Trucks & Tractors

Motorcycles

The Need for Speed

Off-Road Racing

The Pit Crew

Rockcrawling

Rusty Wallace

Stunt Driving

Tony Stewart

The Unsers

STUNT DRIVING

Tara Baukus Mello

An imprint of Infobase Publishing

Chelsea House
An imprint of Infobase Publishing
132 West 31st Street
New York NY 10001

ISBN-10: 0-7910-8666-6
ISBN-13: 978-0-7910-8666-7

Library of Congress Cataloging-in-Publication Data
Mello, Tara Baukus.
  Stunt driving / Tara Baukus Mello.
    p. cm. – (Race car legends. Collector's edition)
Includes bibliographical references and index.
ISBN 0-7910-8666-6 (hardcover)
1. Stunt driving—Juvenile literature. 2. Stunt performers—Juvenile literature. I. Title. II. Series: Race car legends. Collector's edition.
TL152.58.M45 2006   791.43'028—dc22
2005021143

Chelsea House books are available at special discounts when purchased in bulk quantities for businesses, associations, institutions, or sales promotions. Please call our Special Sales Department in New York at (212) 967-8800 or (800) 322-8755.

You can find Chelsea House books on the World Wide Web at http://www.chelseahouse.com

Series design by Erika K. Arroyo
Cover design by Hierophant Publishing Services/EON PreMedia/Joo Young An

Printed in the United States of America

Bang PH 10 9 8 7 6 5 4 3 2 1

This book is printed on acid-free paper.

All links and Web addresses were checked and verified to be correct at the time of publication. Because of the dynamic nature of the Web, some addresses and links may have changed since publication and may no longer be valid.

CONTENTS

1

WELCOME TO THE STUNT DRIVER'S WORLD

There is nothing that compares to watching an action-packed scene on television or in a movie theater. Viewers sit on the edges of their seats, just waiting to see what happens next. Will the bad guys outrun the cops? Will the hero crash and be hurt? High-speed car chases, spectacular crashes, and thrilling jumps—they are all in a day's work for a stunt person. It's a job that may seem glamorous to the casual observer. Others may think that to perform stunts, a person must be a daredevil or have a death wish. Yet both are untrue.

Being a stuntman or stuntwoman requires training and solid skills. Everything is calculated carefully so that no one—the stunt person, the crew, or other actors—gets hurt. The job is far from glamorous. A stunt person often spends hours waiting to be called to perform. That can be pretty boring. Although the action may last just a few moments, the thrill of performing a stunt well is exciting.

Stuntwoman Debbie Evans makes a dramatic motorcycle jump through flames as she doubles for Jamie Lee Curtis in a cell phone commercial.

DOUBLE, SO THERE'S NO TROUBLE

Debbie Evans has been a stuntwoman for more than 28 years and she specializes in car and motorcycle driving stunts. If you've seen *Herbie: Fully Loaded*, *Spider-Man 2*, *Mission Impossible II*, any of the *Fast and Furious* movies, *Inspector Gadget,* or *A Cinderella Story*, then you've seen Evans at work, although you probably didn't know it. Most of the time, Evans is a **stunt double**. A stunt double is a person who performs action scenes for one of the characters in a film and is dressed up to look like the actor he or she is portraying. That means wearing the same clothes and hairstyle, or donning a wig if necessary. It may also mean wearing extra padding or even gaining weight if the actor weighs more than the double. Evans is just one of many stunt people you will meet in this book.

In *Herbie: Fully Loaded*, Evans was the stunt double for Lindsay Lohan, who plays the main character in the movie. Herbie, the Volkswagen Beetle car, has a lot of racing adventures in the movie, and Debbie is behind the wheel in most of them. In one film scene, or sequence, Herbie is competing in a car race. This sequence is really many different scenes that were filmed over several days and put together for the movie. Some of the racing scenes were filmed during the laps of two real races: one that is called the Target House 300, and another called the Pop Secret 500. In these scenes, the real professional racers were driving their own cars. This is why race car drivers such as Dale Earnhardt Jr., Jeff Gordon, and Rusty Wallace have credits as actors in the movie.

The *Herbie* sequence is also mixed in with shots that appear as if these professional racers are driving the cars,

FEARLESS, NOT FOOLISH

Stunt performers are not daredevils. Stuntmen and stuntwomen work hard to be sure the stunts are performed according to a strict plan.

Whether they are falling out of a window, crashing a car, or being set on fire, people who perform stunts professionally have had many hours of training and experience. They want to make sure that they not only do their jobs well, but also without serious injury. "I always take the fall that's going to be the toughest, which means I always expect to come home from work sore, but I never expect to come home broken," explains stuntman Gary Davis.

It may have looked like it was Devon Aoki *(top)* burning up the roads in *2 Fast 2 Furious*, but it was really stunt double Debbie Evans *(bottom)* driving and triggering the flames in the Honda S-2000.

Debbie Evans poses next to *Herbie* during a break in filming NASCAR race scenes. Note the helmet with its built-in Lindsay Lohan wig.

but sometimes there are stunt people driving what look like the real race cars. Mike Ryan was one of the *Herbie* stuntmen who was driving in place of the professional race car drivers in the scene on the California Speedway in Fontana, California. Evans's and Ryan's work on *Herbie: Fully Loaded* will be discussed more later on in the book.

GETTING IN ON THE ACTION

A stunt person who actually plays a character in a film or television program is called a stunt actor. A stunt actor

Stuntman Mark Chadwick starts the action in *Daylight* by driving his car into the Lincoln Tunnel and causing an explosion.

usually looks much like he or she does in real life and sometimes has a speaking role. Stunt actors often appear in television commercials and sometimes have small roles in feature films. Stuntman Mark Chadwick was one of the main stunt drivers in the movie *Daylight* starring Sylvester Stallone. Chadwick plays a jewel thief who drives the car that, in the opening scene of the movie, sets off an explosion that seals a highway tunnel. In this movie, Chadwick is a stunt actor. The audience can see his face clearly and he has a few speaking lines. Filming for the movie's opening scenes alone took two months on both New York City streets and a movie set in Italy.

Mark Chadwick gives an acceptance speech after winning "Best Fire (stunt)" at the 5th Annual Taurus World Stunt Awards in September 2005. Chadwick acts as both a stunt performer and a stunt coordinator.

Because stunt people know that the work they do is dangerous, they do everything they can to make sure they don't get hurt. That means that they have to feel comfortable with all the people who are working behind the scenes setting up stunts, as well as any other stunt people with whom they will be working.

When Debbie Evans was hired for the movie *Mission Impossible II*, the stunt coordinator asked her with whom she wanted to work in a driving stunt where two cars had to look as if they were trying to push each other off the road. It was a dangerous stunt, filmed on a real canyon road with a mountain on one side and a cliff on the other. Both cars were convertibles. One wrong move meant that Evans could get seriously hurt. She chose stuntman Corey Eubanks, who has been performing driving stunts for nearly 30 years.

It is true that there is a risk of getting hurt in any stunt, but those risks are calculated. This means that the stunt person has learned the skills required to do the stunt and is familiar with the type of equipment that is being used. It also means that there are many safety measures and equipment in place during the stunt. For example, in *Daylight*, Mark Chadwick had to sideswipe, or scrape against the driver's door of a car driven by a fellow stuntman. The crew placed foam padding on the inside of the door so the driver would be protected in case the door was pushed in too far.

In a scene in *The Fast and the Furious*, Evans drives a Honda Civic under a moving semitruck and then rolls the car over. This stunt was filmed in several shots. For the rollover shot, the car was outfitted with a steel **roll cage**,

Debbie Evans drives a Corvette under a semitruck in *Never Too Young To Die*, a stunt she later repeated with a Honda Civic in the movie *The Fast and the Furious*.

like the cages used in professional racing. As an added safety measure, the gas tank was removed and replaced with a special tank that wouldn't explode during the rollover. Evans wore a helmet and special restraints to

BOND BREAKS WORLD RECORD

The 2006 blockbuster film *Casino Royale* not only broke the mold with fresh-faced actor Daniel Craig as the new 007, it also used its signature, fast-paced stunt scenes to set a new Guinness World Record. The record-breaking scene involves James Bond's famous Aston Martin flipping seven times in a single take. That is one more roll than ever before. The stunt was performed by Craig's stunt double Adam Kirley.

"We rehearsed the stunt several times driving test cars, which were a similar weight to the Aston Martin, at 80 mph towards a 10 inch ramp. That worked very well, causing the cars to flip over at least five times in rehearsal," co-stunt coordinator Gary Powell told the United Kingdom's Press Association. "But we knew, due to the design and suspension of the Aston Martin DBS, it would probably level itself out in mid-air. When we came to filming the stunt on the night, as suspected, the Aston Martin DBS leveled itself out in mid-air refusing to flip over," he said.

Precision was necessary in perfecting the stunt. Kirley had to drive the Aston at a high speed and release the car at exactly the right moment to perform the record number of rolls.

stop her arms from flying out the windows. She also wore a foam collar and restraints so her neck couldn't move too far in the crash. Then she placed protective pads on her chest, around her back, and on the lower part of her legs. Finally, she had a five-point racing harness for a safety belt, which was so tight she could hardly breathe.

The people described in this book are experienced stunt performers. In addition to driving cars, many do all different kinds of stunts. They can fall off buildings, be set on fire, fight with other stunt people, appear to drown, and more. Because car chases, jumps, crashes, and other car stunts are extremely dangerous, a stunt person must be a highly trained driver.

2

TRAINING

The first step in becoming a professional stunt driver is learning the skills to perform stunts. Learning those skills is just like learning to do anything else—a person needs someone to teach him or her, and the beginner needs a lot of practice. This may sound easy, but often it is not. First, a stunt driver must learn all the techniques required to handle many types of vehicles under different road conditions, such as a wet or snow-covered road. Once he or she masters these skills, the person must learn how to perform stunts such as driving within inches of another car or the film camera, spinning the car, or making a jump.

PRACTICE MAKES PERFECT

Once the skills are mastered, practice is very important. It is through practice that the person learns how to perform the stunt correctly. This means doing the same thing over and over again to perfection, and to **hit the mark** every time. The person must know how to do the stunt without getting hurt, or hurting any other people or breaking equipment on the set. It does not take a lot of training to learn how to do many vehicle stunts. What does take skill

18

A student driver executes a turn on a water-soaked course as part of a vehicle handling drill. Performing a stunt on a slippery surface requires skills that are developed through many hours of practice. In order to maintain control while speeding around a corner on a wet road, for example, a stunt driver must use special driving techniques to compensate for the tires' loss of traction. Once a technique is learned, it must be practiced again and again so a predictable result can be achieved.

and practice is consistently placing the car where it needs to be, until the director has the shot he wants.

To learn how to handle a car under all types of circumstances, many stunt drivers take high-performance driving courses. These courses are often taught at racing schools, but most of the time the students drive a regular car instead of a race car. Participants wear safety gear and drive on a course instead of on a street. These courses are also designed to teach participants how to be better daily drivers. Two of the best-known schools are run by former racers Bob Bondurant and Skip Barber. Both of these schools offer performance driving as well as racing classes.

The first thing students learn in class is vehicle dynamics, which teaches the driver how to best operate the car in any driving situation. For example, students learn about traction, or how much each tire grips the road. They learn that when driving straight and at a steady speed, there is equal weight on each side of the car, and therefore equal traction at each tire. As soon as a driver turns a corner, the weight of the car is shifted to one side, and the car has less traction on one side and more traction on the other.

Many drivers know about vehicle dynamics from everyday driving. Still, a good driving course explains how vehicle dynamics work so drivers will know how to

An instructor at the Bob Bondurant School of High-Performance Driving teaches a group of student drivers how to maintain and regain control of a vehicle in the classroom, before they implement what they learned on the driving course.

respond when they need to make a sudden move. Drivers are also taught what to do if they begin to lose control of the car. By understanding vehicle dynamics, drivers are less likely to lose control, and if they do, they will know how to steady the car.

"The philosophy of going fast is starting slow," said senior instructor Bruce MacInness of the Skip Barber Driving School, which has five locations in the United States. "If it feels fast, you need to slow down." Oversteering is one condition that can cause drivers to feel as if they are moving too fast and out of control. In oversteering, the rear tires have less traction than the front ones, and they begin to slide. If a driver doesn't know how to correct this, the car might spin.

The Skip Barber Driving School uses skid pads, which are sections of pavement that have been made wet and extra slippery, so that participants can learn how to control a skidding vehicle. At the Bob Bondurant School of High-Performance Driving in Phoenix, Arizona, students can drive a "skid" car. This vehicle looks like a spider on wheels. At both schools, an instructor rides with the student and guides him or her through the course. "The biggest challenge [for instructors] is getting the student to look where he wants to end up," said Mike McGovern, chief instructor at the Bob Bondurant School. "You simply need to look at a point of reference and your hands and feet will guide the car there."

In a stunt driver's world, the goal might be to get the car to spin around. First, however, the driver must understand how to get the car back in control during a spin. Once the driver can stop a car from spinning, he or she can be in control when intentionally spinning the car. It is

A student learns how to control skids and swerves by driving a special vehicle called a skid car. The skid car sits on a four-wheeled platform that controls the weight of the car, reducing the tires' contact with the ground on either the front or rear of the car. As a result, the student driver learns to not oversteer or understeer the car.

very important to be in control during the stunt, not only for safety reasons but also to successfully complete each stunt-driving assignment. This means stopping the spin at the right point or keeping the spin going if that is what the film or TV director wants.

Another assignment might be for a stunt person to drive right alongside a **camera car**, keeping a steady speed while heading straight toward another camera. Then, he or she must to swerve at the last moment to avoid hitting the camera. All of this requires a good understanding of vehicle dynamics. These are all the same skills that the driving schools teach on how to avoid an accident. They have just been adapted for the purposes of stunt driving.

EDUCATION BY EXPERIENCE

Many stuntmen and stuntwomen receive an informal education from more experienced drivers. Mike Ryan, a stunt driver who has worked on many films, including *Herbie: Fully Loaded*, started learning his trade more than 30 years ago from a more experienced stuntman. He compared his learning experience to getting a college education, saying that it took him about six years to really master all the techniques needed to be a good stunt driver. "When you are performing a stunt, nothing can happen by chance. You have to have the skills to make it work safely and look good for the camera," he said.

The Bob Bondurant School also has a special class to teach people stunts such as how to push another car out of the way. People who take this class are not only stunt drivers, but also sometimes chauffeurs for famous people who might need to be protected from terrorists or kidnappers. In this class, the student drives a car called the shark, which has a special cage around the front so it can be used again and again. Then, with the instructor by his side, the student learns how to hit a second vehicle to make it spin without damaging the shark. These techniques, called **take outs** and **ramming**, are frequently seen in films or on television.

Back when many of today's most experienced stunt drivers were learning the business, there were no schools for them to attend. Instead, they learned from other, more experienced stunt people. Today, some of the most experienced drivers have opened stunt-driving schools, which give new drivers the necessary experience and allow

Stunt drivers and chauffeurs of famous people who might have to protect their clients though aggressive driving learn how to ram another vehicle in a special car called the shark. The Bob Bondurant School devised the shark with a reinforced bumper so that it could repeatedly ram other cars without getting damaged.

experienced drivers to practice their stunts in a safe environment away from onlookers.

At Bobby Ore's Motion Picture Stunt Driving School in Sebring, Florida, stunt people can learn to perform some intense vehicle stunts. The school concentrates on teaching students actions such as forward and backward 180-degree and 360-degree spins, as well as weaving around orange highway cones both in forward and reverse, and making 90-degree turns.

An aerial view of the Bob Bondurant School in Phoenix, Arizona, shows how 60 acres were developed with various driving courses. Novice drivers as well as seasoned stunt drivers need tracks like these where they can learn and practice in safety.

Rick Seaman's Motion Picture Driving Clinic in Los Angeles, California, is another school popular with stunt drivers. Seaman, who has worked as a stuntman for more than 30 years, has performed stunts in movies including *Charlie's Angels*, *The Adventures of Rocky & Bullwinkle*, and *Inspector Gadget*. At his stunt driving school, Seaman and his team of instructors teach students how to stop a car's rear wheels from spinning (called "locking" the wheels), which makes the vehicle slide and turn. The clinic also teaches students how to perform a "skid-turn," in which they drive a car backwards at high speed, make it spin 180-degrees, and then continue in the same direction moving forward. In some of Seaman's classes, students get to coordinate their own car chases and then drive in them with other students.

These techniques are the foundation for being a stunt driver. Although none of these skills are difficult to learn, they can be hard to do well every time. In addition, many stunts seen on camera are a combination of maneuvers, which makes them even more difficult to do successfully. Sometimes even experienced stunt drivers take these stunt driving courses multiple times to practice their skills.

3

BEHIND THE SCENES

Filming a stunt or a driving sequence takes a long time. What appears for less than one minute on film can take hours, days, and even weeks to make. It requires dozens of people working behind the scenes to make sure everything works the way it is supposed to and as smoothly as possible.

PRE-FILM PREPARATION

Preparations for putting together a stunt begin long before the actual filming starts. First, the director works with someone to explain his vision of how the stunt will look on film. That person, either a lower-level director (called a second-unit or assistant director) or the stunt coordinator, decides how to make the action happen. If a location for the filming hasn't been chosen, it is done at this time.

Then the stunt coordinator hires the people he or she wants to use for the stunt. Those up for selection may need to audition, especially if the jobs require some acting or reading script lines. They may just be selected based on their experience in doing a particular stunt. For example,

27

only a few stunt people are experienced at "skiing" a car—driving a car on just the two wheels of either the driver's side or passenger's side.

While the stunt people are being selected, other preparations are also taking place. Sometimes the script calls for a certain type of vehicle, and so the appropriate cars need to be chosen. Depending on the complexity of the stunt, several look-alike cars may be used. In *Herbie: Fully Loaded*, for example, there were 36 different "Herbie" Volkswagens. For each type of stunt, the car must be specially prepared. A car that is going to jump must be prepared differently than a car that is going to be rolled. Even in a single scene, two identical cars with different preparations will be used if the stunt requires the car first to jump and then later to roll.

Almost all cars that will be performing many different kinds of stunts will have some similar features. For example, most of the time a special small gas tank, called a fuel cell, is installed in place of the regular gas tank. The fuel cell only provides enough gas to perform the stunt. This helps keep the stunt person safe if there is a fire or explosion, because there will only be a small amount of gas in the car.

A five-point safety harness, like the ones that race car drivers use, often takes the place of a regular seat belt. Even in a shot where a driver is visible in the car, viewers may not see the safety harness because it is probably hidden under his or her clothing. Then, depending on how dangerous the stunt is, a roll cage might be installed in the car. This is a frame constructed of thick steel tubing that protects the driver from injury. The device is similar to a roll cage that is installed in a race car. The stunt driver's

A few of Herbie's secrets are revealed in these pictures.
Herbie can perform a perfect wheelie by using either a
counterweight *(top)*, or hydraulic lift *(bottom)*. The movie is
edited so that the viewer does not see these modifications
to the car. Notice how difficult it is for the driver to see
over the hood of this specially prepared stunt car.

Debbie Evans poses inside the roll cage installed in "NASCAR" Herbie. She wears a safety harness and helmet to protect her from injury.

seat is sometimes modified or has a special cushion added to protect the driver from impact when the stunt is performed. In many stunts, especially car rolls or jumps, there is a danger that the stunt person could injure or even break his or her back.

Stunt driver Richard Ziker broke his back while filming a movie stunt. The film was *The Darwin Awards*, about the Internet awards given to individuals who do reckless, dangerous stunts that cause them harm or even death. Ziker was performing a stunt in which he was to drive a 1967 car off the side of a cliff. Before the stunt, he checked the car thoroughly to make sure that it was in good shape and could support him in the stunt. He

PLANNING MAKES PERFECT

Before stunt performers are able to rehearse a scene, the stunt coordinator must make sure that the drivers, crew, and cameramen understand each of the sequences. There are two strategies that most stunt coordinators use today. The first strategy is to demonstrate the scene using miniature cars. The stunt coordinator moves and places the cars in the correct spots for the different camera shots. Another frequently used method of planning stunts is creating a **storyboard**—a series of sketches demonstrating each part of a stunt, allowing the stunt coordinator to visualize each scene ahead of time.

thought everything looked good, but when he performed the stunt, the car landed in a soft patch of sand and the entire rear end of the car fell apart when it hit the ground. "What looked like solid metal [under the car] was really just a thin shell, so I had no way of knowing that the car wouldn't stand up to the gag," Ziker said.

Preparations must also be made for vehicles used in live stunts that you see in theme parks or on some reality television shows. Stuntman Rick Seaman prepares all the cars for stunts that contestants perform on the NBC television show *Fear Factor*. On the show, each contestant completes an identical stunt, competing against each other until a winner is selected. For vehicle stunts, it appears as if each contestant uses the same vehicle for the stunt, but this is rarely the case. "Sometimes we have as many as 12 cars," explained Seaman.

Because the contestants who perform stunts on *Fear Factor* are not stunt professionals, extra care is taken to

A camera *(upper right of picture)* captures a stunt on the TV show *Fear Factor* where a participant stands on a car that is held in mid-air by a giant magnet. Various rigging, safety lines and guidelines are used to keep the car under control and the contestant safe.

reduce the possibility of injury. In one episode, contestants had to jump a convertible car into a small pond, and then get out of the car and swim to a platform. Jumping into water is very dangerous, even for a stuntman. Seaman took many precautions as he put together the stunt. First, he used cars that originally had hard tops, instead of real convertibles, so he could strengthen the area around the windshield with special tubing to prevent collapse. Then, he replaced the windshield glass with a special plastic called Lexan so it wouldn't break when it hit the water. Next, he needed to make sure that when the contestants jumped the car, the front of the car would hit first, but not in a way that might make it flip over. He built a special ramp to do this and then added a **counterweight** in the trunk.

In most *Fear Factor* stunts, the contestants wear a lot of safety gear, but in this stunt they could not wear too much. If they did, it would have been hard for them to swim away from the car. Instead of wearing pads to protect them during the stunt, Seaman glued the pads all over the inside of the car. Then there were two safety divers in the water.

When the stunt was completely **rigged**, it was tested twice before it was considered safe for the contestants. "In this stunt, like with all *Fear Factor* stunts, every measure is taken to make sure the contestants are safe," Seaman said.

One of the most complex stunt vehicles to prepare is an 18-wheel semitruck. Mike Ryan, a stuntman for more than 30 years, is well known for his stunts with semitrucks and tractor-trailers. Because these vehicles are so big and so heavy, there is a much greater risk to cameras,

This tanker is being prepared by Mike Ryan and his production crew to perform a stunt. Cameras are mounted on the outside of the cab to capture action that happens inside the cab.

crewmembers, and the driver when performing a stunt. It is also much more difficult to actually perform a stunt in this type of vehicle.

Because Ryan has so much experience with these types of stunts, he knows what to do to get the effect the director wants. This might mean using different tires, changing how much air is in the tires, or a combination of adjustments. For safety reasons, parts that might come loose during a stunt are attached securely with chains. A double roll-cage and a special seat are sometimes used, depending on the stunt.

Although much is done in advance of filming a stunt, some preparations must be made the day before the shoot or even right before shooting begins. Ramps for jumps or rolls need to be moved into position. To make the landing a bit softer on the driver, sometimes a portable "pit" is placed where the vehicle is supposed to land. The pit might be filled with sand or another substance to cushion the landing. Other times a mountain of cardboard boxes is used to cushion a vehicle's landing.

If the car is supposed to explode or catch on fire, then the second-unit director or the stunt coordinator works with the special-effects crew to tell them where to put the explosives. If the director wants to get a certain camera angle, but it is too dangerous for a camera operator to stay with the camera, a remote-controlled camera is used. This camera might be placed in a special enclosure so it will not be damaged if the car runs into it.

READY TO ROLL CAMERAS

When the stunt people arrive for the day of shooting, they report to the wardrobe department to see if they need to wear any special clothing. Next, they go to the makeup department. Once they are ready, they check in with the stunt coordinator and are given their assignments. The coordinator then conducts a series of rehearsals and discusses what is going to happen, as well as what to do if something unexpected happens. Stunts are precisely planned with split-second timing. Sometimes the stunt driver takes charge and lays out his own plans.

A remote controlled camera is set up to film the action from ground level as a tanker driven by Mike Ryan wraps around a car *(top)*, and ultimately jackknifes, smashing the car and taking the camera out with it *(bottom)*.

Once briefed, all the stunt people get in their vehicles and rehearse at a speed that is slower than what will actually be performed on film. A **half-speed** rehearsal is not performed literally at half of the speed of the actual performance. It is usually much slower than that. If the stunt is being done on city streets, then hired police officers block other traffic from entering the area. This rehearsal gives everyone a clear picture of what will happen, so there is less risk of something going wrong during filming. This is the time when crew and coordinator look for potential problems, such as anything distracting in the background.

If a change is necessary, the coordinator may call the stunt people back into a meeting, at which time he or she demonstrates the stunt sequence again, with the new changes. Then everyone goes back to another half-speed rehearsal. Once everything is set, each stunt person goes to his or her starting point, or first position, and waits for the director to call "Action!"

4

PRECISION DRIVING

One aspect of stunt driving is called precision driving, or performance driving. This is the type of driving most often seen in commercials, although all stunt driving has elements of precision driving mixed into it. The easiest way to tell that a scene only involves precision driving is if the vehicle does not crash, jump, or roll. Car chases sometimes require only precision driving. Precision driving is also used if just one car is being filmed.

Often television commercials for cars show only one car. It might be a truck skidding on a highway, a convertible going down a curvy wet road, or a sport utility vehicle driving off-road. Just because only one car is shown does not necessarily make the driving any easier. This is where the precision part comes into play. The driver still needs to hit the mark, sometimes coming within inches of a camera or a camera car. He or she also needs to drive at a steady speed. It is not as easy as it sounds, especially if the stunt driver has never driven that specific car before, or if the shot calls for high-speed maneuvering.

Drivers must possess precision driving skills in order to perform a stunt like the one shown in this scene from *2 Fast 2 Furious*. In this example, the drivers must drive at a steady rate of speed while consistently maintaining a small distance between vehicles.

In a series of commercials for Chevrolet, stuntman Mike Ryan drove a semitruck carrying a load of cars in its carrier. In the commercials, 10 different new cars, including a Corvette and a bright yellow Chevrolet SSR, drive on or off the car carrier while it is cruising down the highway. In order for the other stunt performers to drive on or off the car carrier safely, it was critical that

Ryan drove both at a steady speed and stayed in the very center of the lane.

The weight of the car carrier, the vehicles it was carrying, and the road were all factors Ryan had to consider. Sometimes these items changed as the scene was being shot. For example, in one scene, several stunt drivers drove off the top of the car carrier one at a time. This meant that Ryan had to change how he was driving in reaction to their movement and the changes in the weight of the semitruck's load.

This city street has been closed for the filming of a car commercial. To emulate traffic, precision drivers maintain their cars a steady pace alongside a new car carrier. A camera truck leads the procession with the crew filming the vehicles behind it.

Since a lot of precision-driving work is done for commercials for automobile manufacturers, the cars and scenery must be appealing. Location scouts often choose beautiful locations on curving roads that wind through mountains or along the water. Of course the car also must look beautiful on film, and the stunt driver has to perform certain actions to help ensure that the car looks its best.

As soon as the stunt driver gets in the car, he or she puts on the seat belt. Since it is likely that this action will be seen in the final commercial, it is very important to do. It sets a good example for viewers watching. Next, the car doors are locked and the windows are rolled up all the way. Many cars have door locks that can be seen from the outside of the vehicle, and commercial makers believe that the car looks better if the locks are down.

When filming starts, the driver sees to it that the radio and air-conditioning are off. Although viewers would not be able to hear the music, many times an antenna shoots up when the radio is on. That is something else that commercial makers think looks bad on screen. Having the air-conditioning turned off can sometimes make it hot for the driver, but it is necessary. Air-conditioning units cause water droplets to gather under the vehicle, which sometimes makes it appear as if something is leaking from car.

Before filming begins, the driving sequence is rehearsed to check the lighting and the background. The director is also checking the positioning of the vehicle and making decisions, for example, on which stretch of road looks best. Many times, a crewmember drives the car during this part of the preparation. Once everything has been decided, the stunt driver goes for a **dry run**. In this

In a commercial, dramatic landscape and perfect lighting combined with precision driving show off a car to its best advantage.

rehearsal, everything happens exactly the way it will happen during the filming. Everyone is in position, including the camera people and the camera car, although they are not necessarily filming yet.

The people who are behind the camera during filming often must be precision drivers, too. Rick Miller is a stuntman who has acted as a precision driver both in front of and behind the camera. He has built several camera bikes, which are motorcycles designed to hold small cameras. Miller rides his camera bikes to get the shots the director wants. While Miller is doing that, the cameraman stands on the sidelines and operates the camera using a remote control. Sometimes Miller chases a vehicle at very close range.

A camera bike films a chase scene at close range in *Matrix Reloaded*, creating a real feeling of speed for the viewer.

Other times he might ride straight toward two cars, then ride in between them. "You get a much better sense of speed when the camera is mounted on a moving vehicle than when it is parked on the side of the road," explained Miller.

Although precision driving is most often seen in commercials, it also appears on television programs and in movies. Sometimes the director uses precision driving to create tension in a story by creating a series of "near misses" before the final stunt. Other times, precision driving is done in between stunts. For example, a car might weave in and out of traffic, sideswiping one or two cars but avoiding all others.

STAGING A STUNT

During a dry run, the driver must learn how to hit the mark and must figure out how to communicate well with the crew. The driver determines how far to back up in order to reach the director's desired speed. If the first image requires the car to come from around a corner, the driver may beep the horn or speak into a handheld radio to inform the crew to roll the cameras. If the sequence requires the stunt person to drive next to a camera car, then the driver may use a mark on the car, such as the edge of the windshield wiper to make sure the car stays the same distance from the camera at all times. Usually, there are several dry runs, and after each, the stuntman goes back to his or her starting place.

AT THE MOVIES

One car chase scene that required a lot of precision driving was in *Mission Impossible II*. The main female character, played by Thandie Newton, is chasing the main male character, played by Tom Cruise, on a winding road. Debbie Evans acted as a stunt double for Newton and performed all the driving for that sequence. In the scene, Evans had to bump into the lead car several times, as if she were trying to push the car off the road. This was a challenge because Evans had to be careful to not hit the other car so hard that she caused serious damage. Yet she also had to make the scene look realistic.

One part of the scene called for Evans to nearly miss colliding head-on with another car. This was particularly dangerous because the road that they were filming on had a mountain on one side and a cliff with a 600-foot drop on the other. Because of the traction control system, Evans had a hard time locking up the brakes to slide out of the way. "Fortunately I hit a slight embankment and I stopped. That was all that protected me from the cliff," she said.

At the end of the scene, the two cars get stuck together side-by-side and spin around multiple times before they nearly slide off the road and over the cliff. It is not possible for two cars to connect like that in real life, so the stunt coordinator had to figure out another way to make this happen. To complete the spinning part of the stunt, the crew built a rotating platform, which was mounted on a track that was hidden under the road. The cars were then positioned on the turntable, which was slid along the track until it stopped at the edge of the cliff. Because this did not require any driving skills, the stunt performers took a break and the two lead actors played their own parts for that scene.

Another time that precision driving is used is in live action shows in front of an audience. In one show, Jeremy Fry was one of five stunt drivers who performed a live show on the deck of the USS *Midway* aircraft carrier. Each performer was driving a convertible Porsche Boxster and the cars had to interact with each other in different formations, like birds flying in the air. The live show lasted only eight minutes, but the team spent three days rehearsing all of the driving routines. In one formation, four of the cars were moving forward at the same time and Fry wove his car through them. In another move, the cars stopped in front of the audience and then Fry slid his car in between the cars and the audience and drove off.

Because the cars were convertibles, all the drivers could hear the audience's reactions as they performed. "Live shows are fun because you get instant feedback from the crowd, but there's also a lot of pressure because there's no take two. It has to be right the first time," said Fry.

5

STUNT DRIVING

Stunt driving is a very broad category that covers many types of driving for commercials, television, and movies. It includes the simplest stunts, such as two cars crashing, as well as the most complex actions, such as multiple cars crashing, rolling, or exploding. In the stunt business, the more complex a stunt is, the more people it takes to create it, the more time it takes to perform it, and the more money it costs to produce. A major motion picture with very complex stunt sequences could cost well over a million dollars. A stunt-driving sequence may only last a few seconds on film, but each stunt requires careful preparation, rehearsal, and then hours of filming to get exactly the right shot.

Many times stunt driving combines precision-driving techniques with more dangerous stunts. In the movie *Lethal Weapon 4*, the two lead characters, played by Mel Gibson and Danny Glover, are chasing a villain on the highway. A collision with the villain's car causes them to lose control, run off a raised part of a highway, and crash into the third story of an office building. Then they drive through the office building and crash out the other side, landing back on another section of the raised highway.

A driver crashes a car through a second story window in a scene from *Knock Off*. In this stunt, it is important that the driver hit the glass at the right rate of speed, and that he stay in the center of the window.

Stuntman Henry Kingi Sr. drove the car for this crash scene. It takes about one minute in the final film, but it took days of planning and rehearsal to get it right. Rick Seaman was one of the stunt people in the film, and he also helped stunt coordinator Conrad Palmisano put together the action. The stunt was actually done in four different parts: the car leaving the highway, the car jumping into the third story of the office building, the car crashing out of the building, and the car landing on the other highway. Then these scenes were pieced together with close-up shots of the actors in the car and the office workers running out of the way, which made it even more dramatic.

What is amazing about this stunt is that all the actions that viewers see on film are not special effects—they all really took place. The building is really an office building and the car really jumped through the large glass window on the third story, drove through the building, and crashed out the other side. Jumping a car 50 feet in the air and crashing through a window that is 11 square feet requires absolute precision. If Kingi had not hit the jump fast enough, he wouldn't have hit the window with enough power to travel through it, or he could have missed it entirely. If he were off a little bit to the right or the left, he would hit the steel columns that supported the building and most likely injure himself. To rehearse the stunt, the team did a test at ground level with an identical car and the same jump. They built a wooden goalpost the same size as the window for Kingi to jump through.

When Kingi drove the car through the office, all the people in the scene were stunt people who knew how to safely get out of the car's way while still making it look as if they were in danger. The window washers, who dove out of the way as the car crashed through the window on the other side, were also stunt people. When the car exited the building, it did not land on the highway, as the movie shows. "When Henry came out the third story window, he landed in a mountain of cardboard boxes that was two stories high, designed to cushion his landing," explained Seaman. "When he landed, it didn't even dent the car."

Piles of cardboard boxes are often used to cushion the landings of stunt vehicles.

Sometimes a stunt driver works with another stunt person who is outside the vehicle. One of the most frequently seen stunts of this type is when a driver hits a pedestrian. Usually the stunt person playing the pedestrian is actually hit. However, the two stunt people make sure that the scene is done in such a way that the pedestrian does not actually get hurt. To get the timing down while still being safe, both stunt people practice the stunt over and over at increasingly higher speeds.

Cheryl Bermeo, a stuntwoman who has performed this type of action said, "We worked together, first talking about how I would hit the car and then practicing it.

FILMING MADE SIMPLE

Stuntman Cotton Mather is the creator of a special motorcycle camera vehicle called Moto Cam. It is a Yamaha motorcycle with a sidecar. The sidecar is a tiny car with an additional wheel that is attached to the side of the motorcycle. The Moto Cam's sidecar was custom-made for camera operators and equipment. Its two seats are like those in race cars, with one seat facing forward and one facing backward. With this arrangement, a camera operator can film from either direction or from both directions at the same time. Both seats have five-point racing harnesses so that the operators can't be thrown out of the seats. The car has also been modified to accommodate the sidecar and the extra weight of the camera crew and their equipment. Because of the sidecar, the Moto Cam steers more like a car than a motorcycle, allowing it to follow the movements of another vehicle more easily. This makes the final filmed sequence more believable to the audience.

We started at five miles per hour and slowly worked up to me taking the hit at the speed the script called for—fifteen miles per hour." Because this stunt can be especially tricky, Bermeo and the stunt driver looked at the car they were using to figure out where she should place her hands and how she would roll off the front of the car. Timing is very important in this stunt because Bermeo had to react quickly enough to jump up slightly so that the initial impact of the car was not so severe.

In many stunts, timing is one of the key factors that makes the stunt look good. But proper timing is also an important way to reduce the danger to the stunt people. In one scene in *Batman Begins*, stuntman Rick Miller is in a

A stuntman takes a hit in *The Living Daylights*. This stunt must be practiced over and over at increasing speeds in order to get the timing right to prevent injury.

police car that is chasing the Batmobile through a tunnel. The Batmobile is shooting firebombs out its back and one of them causes a tire on Miller's car to blow up. He loses control and his car goes sideways. Then another police car hits his door, causing his car to roll over. Miller's car lands on its roof and slides about 100 feet before stopping.

This stunt was filmed in a real tunnel in Chicago. Because this was a real tunnel, everything inside the tunnel was also real, instead of being made of foam and other soft substances that would be used in a tunnel built just for the movie. "Because the tunnel was only 25 feet wide and had cement columns on the sides, I had to put the car exactly in the middle of the tunnel when I slid sideways in order for the stunt to work," said Miller.

The timing for this stunt was very important because if Miller and the other driver didn't hit their marks at the right times, the stunt would not be believable. To help make sure the stunt went smoothly, the stunt team rehearsed it multiple times in a parking lot. They used cones to recreate the tunnel. They also measured each part of the stunt to determine the speeds the vehicles needed to travel. They knew that if just one person's timing was off, the entire stunt would fall apart and someone might get hurt. "No matter how many times you do a stunt like this, it's never a piece of cake," said Miller. "There are just too many unknowns."

6

PUTTING IT ALL TOGETHER

If you have ever sat on the edge of your seat during an action-packed scene in your favorite television show or movie, then you know all about stunt sequences. A stunt sequence is made up of a series of different events filmed from different angles. These shots are all pieced together in the editing process to create the director's vision of what the final scene should look like.

There is no right or wrong way to join the different shots, but there are ways to create more suspense. Sometimes you can watch an action scene and your heart starts to beat faster. You grip your seat tightly, hoping the hero is saved from the big disaster. Sometimes, however, an action-packed scene is not all that interesting, even though there are a lot of special effects and plenty of things happening. As with the other scenes in a film, the action sequences begin with the director's idea of how the written script will be put into play on screen. In the end, however, it is up to many people to make sure that vision creates suspense for the audience.

Herbie moves towards the head of the pack in a scene filmed for *Herbie: Fully Loaded*. The NASCAR race sequence was shot over a period of several days. The film was then skillfully edited to make the race appear exciting and believable to the audience.

In order to make any scene believable, the action must be realistic for the character. For example, an extremely elderly man probably would not be racing around on city streets. Yet if the script required him to be driving wildly, the director might create a situation in which someone was chasing the old man, in order to make the dangerous driving believable to the audience.

It might be hard to imagine a tiny, 1963 Volkswagen Beetle competing in, let alone winning, all kinds of races. But in *Herbie: Fully Loaded*, that's exactly what happens. Because of the story, or plot, the audience believes it. In the car racing stunt sequence in the movie, Herbie the Volkswagen wins the race. To make the audience believe that this is possible, Herbie must overcome many challenges. He starts at the back of the pack of cars and slowly works his way up front. At one point he gets surrounded by three other cars that push him into the railing on the side of the racetrack. Eventually, though, Herbie manages to get by all the other race cars and crosses the finish line first.

A camera rig is attached to Herbie's roof for filming scenes with his NASCAR competitors.

The film sequence where Herbie competes in a car race was filmed in many parts during the course of many days. For the part where Herbie is interacting with the other race cars, stuntwoman Debbie Evans was driving Herbie and stunt people drove all the other cars on the track. Because this needed to look like a real race for the film, it was important that the cars drove quite fast. Sometimes Evans was driving at more than 100 miles per hour in the old Volkswagen.

There were many challenges to performing this stunt. Sometimes Evans had to drive within a few inches of the camera car or one of the other cars that appears in the film. When Herbie gets pushed up against the side railing, the sides of the Volkswagen's tires actually touched the edge, burning the rubber. Evans had to perform this stunt several times for the camera, and eventually Herbie's tires got so thin that she needed to put on new tires. If she hadn't checked the tires when she did, she might have had an accident.

In the movie *The Italian Job*, three Mini Coopers are used play an important role in allowing the main characters to get away with a big robbery. There were 32 Mini Coopers that were customized specifically for the movie. Some were **jump cars** designed so they could repeatedly perform the jumps required for the scenes. Other cars were rigged for special effects. For example, the crew replaced the original windows with special glass that would break a certain way when the villains shot at the car. Other cars were reserved as **hero cars**, so they would always be in perfect condition. The driving stunts in the movie are all real. There were no special effects or computer-generated images used. Many times the cars were damaged

In *The Italian Job,* actors Mark Wahlberg, Charlize Theron, and Jason Statham drive Mini Coopers down a flight of stairs into a subway station. The actors attended stunt driving school so that they could perform this scene themselves.

during the stunts. As a result, there was an auto repair shop built just for the movie. The director could send a car there at any time, 24 hours a day, to be fixed so it would be ready for the next day's shooting.

In the turning point of the movie, there are many impressive scenes that included both precision driving and stunt driving. In some of these scenes, the actors performed their own stunts. For example, in the scene where the characters played by Mark Wahlberg, Charlize Theron, and Jason Statham drive three Mini Coopers down a set of stairs and into a subway station in Hollywood, it really is the actors performing in that scene. Another interesting

DECIDING THE DETAILS

Many times, a script does not detail the action but gives only a general description. For example, a script might call for a car accident in which the hero ends up in the hospital. In this case, the director, his or her assistants, and sometimes the stunt coordinator decide how the accident should happen. These decisions are based on a lot of factors, including the budget, the film location, and the director's vision of the film as a whole.

fact about that scene is that the Mini Coopers were not powered by gasoline engines; they were electric. Because this was a real subway station, the gasoline cars would not have been safe. If there had been an accident, a gasoline engine could have exploded and fire could have spread in the enclosed subway. Because there is no electric version of the Mini Cooper, gasoline-powered Mini Coopers had to be converted to electric cars just for that movie.

The lead actors in the movie all went to a stunt driving school so they could perform certain scenes themselves. They spent about three weeks at the school, learning how to do the maneuvers safely. Of course, some of the driving sequences were too challenging or too dangerous for the actors to perform. For these scenes, experienced stunt performers were used.

One scene in the movie was particularly tricky and dangerous. The three Mini Coopers drive through the streets of Los Angeles, chased by a helicopter. There is a lot of precision driving as the three cars weave in and out of traffic. Toward the end of the sequence, a helicopter chases the Mini Cooper driven by Wahlberg's character

Professional stunt drivers did the driving in *The Italian Job* when it came to filming the dangerous helicopter chase scenes.

into a street underneath a cement bridge. Sean Graham, who has acted as Wahlberg's stunt double in other movies, did the driving in this stunt.

Graham and the stunt team rehearsed for about two weeks. It was important that they calculated every moment of the scene between the helicopter and the car because there was no room for error. "The [helicopter's] blades were only about eight feet from the cement underside of the bridge and I had to slide the car under the helicopter," explained Graham. "One wrong move and many people could have been hurt." Even in rehearsals, it was too dangerous to use the helicopter, so the only time the helicopter and the Mini Cooper ever performed together was in the sequence seen in the final film. The scene was all done in one try and every moment is real. "It was one of the most technical stunts I've ever been a part of," said Graham.

In the stunt person's world, everything is made to look realistic and highly dangerous. In real life, however, a stunt person and all the support people on a set have been trained to make sure no one gets hurt. The next time you watch an action-packed driving sequence, look carefully and see if you can identify some of the special techniques that make it so exciting to watch.

CHRONOLOGY

1962 Richard Ziker performs his first stunt.

1977 Debbie Evans performs her first driving stunt on a motorcycle for the television series *ChiPs.*

1990 Sean Graham enters the stunt business.

1993 Rick Miller performs his first stunt.

1996 *Daylight* is released.

1997 Rick Seaman opens his Motion Picture Driving Clinic.

1998 *Lethal Weapon 4* is released.

1999 *Inspector Gadget* hits theaters.

2000 *Charlie's Angels* is released.

2001 *The Fast and The Furious* arrives in theaters.

2003 *The Italian Job* and *2 Fast 2 Furious* are released.

2004 Mike Ryan drives the semi-truck during filming of the Chevrolet commercial series.

2005 *Herbie: Fully Loaded, The Darwin Awards,* and *Batman Begins* are released.

2006 The James Bond movie *Casino Royale* sets a Guinness World Record for car rolls in a single shot.

GLOSSARY

Camera car—Any vehicle, such as a pickup truck, car, motorcycle, or car pulling a trailer, that carries the camera crew and camera equipment.

Counterweight—A weight in one section of the car, such as the trunk, that will make it easier for that part of the vehicle to stay closer to the ground than the rest of the vehicle.

Dry run—Rehearsing a driving sequence before any of the dangerous elements are added, such as a wet road or explosives.

Half-speed—Describing a slow-speed rehearsal of a driving stunt

Hero car—A car identical to the one being used for the stunt. This car is used for close-ups inside the vehicle, such as showing the actor, and in driving scenes that do not involve stunts.

Hit the mark—To be in the proper position at a specific point in the filming.

Jump car—A vehicle that has been specially prepared to make a jump.

Ramming—When one car hits another car hard, then backs off.

Rig—Set up a stunt.

Roll cage—Steel cage inside a car that helps the driver stay in his or her seat and not get injured by a car as it's smashed in any direction.

Storyboard—A diagram that shows the position and movement of the vehicles in a stunt sequence.

Take-out—When one car hits another car, damaging it so it cannot be driven anymore.

BIBLIOGRAPHY

Evans, Debbie. Discussion with the author, April 12, 2005.
Fry, Jeremy. Discussion with the author, April 13, 2005.
Graham, Sean. Discussion with the author, April 18, 2005.
Miller, Rick. Discussion with the author, April 15, 2005.
Seaman, Rick. Discussion with the author, April 13, 2005.
Ziker, Richard. Discussion with the author, April 13, 2005.

FURTHER READING

Bondurant, Bob, and John Blakemore. *Bob Bondurant on High-Performance Driving*. Osceola, Wisc.: Motorbooks International, 1998.

Cooper, Ed J. Gaskell. *Make Your Own Hollywood Movie: A Step-by-Step Guide to Scripting, Storyboarding, Casting, Shooting, Editing, and Publishing Your Very Own Blockbuster Movie*. Alameda, Calif.: Sybex, Inc., 2004.

Parker, Barry. *Death Rays, Jet Packs, Stunts, and Supercars: The Fantastic Physics of Film's Most Celebrated Secret Agent*. Baltimore: Johns Hopkins University Press, 2005.

Turner, Cherie. *Stunt Performers: Life Before The Camera*. New York: Rosen Publishing Group, 2001.

Vinther, Janus. *Special Effects Make-up*. New York: Routledge, 2003.

Weintraub, Aileen. *Stunt Double*. Minneapolis: Sagebrush, 2003.

FILM/DVD

Press, Eric (director). *Behind The Action: Stuntmen in the Movies*. Turner Classic Movies Documentary, 2002.

Barber, Skip. *Going Faster: The Official Visual Guide of the Skip Barber Racing School*. Kultur, 2004.

WEB SITES

www.bobbyoresports.com
Web site for Bobby Ore and his stunt driving school.

www.bondurant.com
Web site for Bob Bondurant and his high performance driving school.

www.imdb.com

International Movie Database Web site, which provides information about feature films and the people who work on them. Access to photos and movie trailers for many films.

www.lacr.net/stunt.html

Web site for Motion Picture Driving Clinic, held at Los Angeles International Raceway.

www.skipbarber.com

Web site for Skip Barber Driving School.

PICTURE CREDITS

INDEX

ABOUT THE AUTHOR

TARA BAUKUS MELLO is a freelance automotive writer. During her 20 years as a writer, she has published more than 3,700 articles in newspapers and magazines. Mello is the author of *Tony Stewart, Rusty Wallace, Mark Martin, The Pit Crew, Stunt Driving,* and *Danica Patrick,* all part of the RACE CAR LEGENDS: COLLECTOR'S EDITION series. A graduate of Harvard University, she lives in southern California, where she cruises the streets in her 1932 Ford pickup street rod that she built with her father.